Revised

101
High Jump Drills

Cliff Rovelto and Gwen Wentland

©2014 Coaches Choice. Revised edition. All rights reserved. Printed in the United States.

No part of this book may be reproduced, stored in a retrieval system or transmitted, in any form or by any means, electronic, mechanical, photocopying, recording, or otherwise, without the prior permission of Coaches Choice. Throughout this book, the masculine shall be deemed to include the feminine and vice versa.

ISBN: 978-1-60679-287-2
Library of Congress Control Number: 2013951345
Cover design & book layout: Cheery Sugabo
Front cover photo: Rod Mikinski
Text photos (unless otherwise noted): Rod Mikinski Photography
(www.mikinskiphotography.com)

Coaches Choice
P.O. Box 1828
Monterey, CA 93942
www.coacheschoice.com

Dedication

To all the coaches and athletes from whom I have learned so much.
—Cliff Rovelto

To Rhoda and Paris—great ones past and present.
—Gwen Wentland

Acknowledgments

Thanks to my wife, Karol, who has always afforded me the time to pursue my passion. Thanks to Gwen Wentland for such a long-standing coach-athlete relationship and for inviting me to co-author this book. Thanks to the coaches who have influenced me tremendously with their teachings, their character, and their professionalism—particularly Bob Knoll, Bob Timmons, and Rick McGuire.

—Cliff Rovelto

I would like to thank my parents, Al and Marie, for allowing me the opportunity to experience, learn, and grow in athletics. I also want to thank my coach and co-author, Cliff Rovelto, for the gift of his time and knowledge. Finally, I would like to thank my husband, Rod Mikinski, for his patience, support, and love.

—Gwen Wentland

Foreword

For over 20 years, Coach Cliff Rovelto has been my close colleague, competitor, collaborator, and friend. My athletes have competed with his on more occasions than they have with any other coach's athletes. And, I am confident that no coach has attended more of Cliff's clinic presentations, or observed him teaching and coaching high jumpers on more occasions than myself. In my opinion, he is the absolute finest coach and teacher of the high jump in America today. His record speaks for itself—no individual has coached more major conference champions, NCAA champions, U.S. national champions, and Olympians.

I have personally learned so much about coaching the high jump from Cliff. He has changed the way I conceptualize and think about the event. His understandings and applications are simple and easy to teach. More important, they are correct and they work. Whenever I have questions about the high jump, or become puzzled by an athlete's lack of progress in the event, I call Cliff.

With Cliff as her coach, Gwen Wentland grew into one of the finest high-jump competitors in United States track and field history. She has done it all, from winning U.S. championships, to competing at the most elite levels of international track and field, including the World Championships. I have long admired Gwen, not only as a great competitor and champion, but also as a terrific young woman and ambassador for our sport.

Here, the team of Cliff Rovelto and Gwen Wentland have joined together to share their knowledge and experiences in this outstanding new text, 101 High Jump Drills. I encourage anyone who is interested in the high jump event, or is interested in teaching and coaching others, or is wishing to jump higher themselves, to read this book and incorporate these great ideas, approaches, and drills into their own training and practice sessions. Both you and your athletes will be pleased that you did. I know that I am.

Dr. Rick McGuire
Head Track and Field Coach
University of Missouri
(2008)

Contents

Dedication 3

Acknowledgments 4

Foreword 5

Introduction 11

Chapter 1: Warm-Up Drills 13

    1   Prisoner Squats

    2   Zombies

    3   Walking With Varying Foot Positions

    4   Speed Skaters

    5   Iron Cross

    6   Scorpion

    7   Egg Shells

    8   Sewing Machine

    9   Forward Low Walks

    10   Running A

    11   Leg Swings

    12   Pretzel Glute Stretch

    13   Dribble With Roundhouse Karate Kick

Chapter 2: Approach Drills 29

    14 Ladder Accelerations

    15 Acceleration Using Resistance

    16 Approaches With Hand Weights

    17 Rhythm Runs

    18 Curve Running

    19 Circles

    20 Figure Eights

    21 Approaches on the High-Jump Apron

    22 Assisted Sprints

    23 "S" Runs

Chapter 3: Takeoff Mechanism Drills 37

    24 Circles With Pop Offs

    25 Long-Jump Takeoffs

    26 Pop Offs Over Low Barriers

    27 Hurdling

    28 Gallop

    29 Oliver Drill With Hurdles

    30 Oliver Drill With One Step

    31 Oliver Drill With Three Steps

    32 One-Box Penultimate

    33 Box-Ground-Box Long Jump Takeoffs With Run-Up

    34 Skipping Takeoffs

    35 Standing Takeoffs With Spot

    36 Three-Step Takeoffs

37 Scissors

   38 High Jump Off an Elevated Surface

Chapter 4: Bar-Clearance Drills 55

   39 Back Overs

   40 Back Overs Off the Ground

   41 Back Overs Off a Box

   42 Run Up Off Two Feet

   43 Wrestler's Arch

Chapter 5: Special Strength Exercises 61

   44 Wheelbarrow

   45 Side-Ups

   46 L-Ups With Push

   47 Diagonals

   48 Partner Exchange With Toss

   49 Hanging Russian Hamstring

   50 Hanging Knee Raises With Medicine Ball

Chapter 6: More Exercises With Weight 71

   51 Overhead Backward Throw

   52 Underhand Forward Throw

   53 Hay Toss Left and Right

   54 Arms—Single Support

   55 Arms—Double Support

   56 Arms—Physioball

   57 Curve Running

   58 Walking Lunges

   59 Takeoffs

    60 Leg Toss

    61 Hamstring Curls

    62 Toss and Catch

    63 Walking Torso Twists

    64 Standing Knee Drive

    65 Back Hypers on a Bench With Toss

    66 Seated Adductor Toss

    67 Seated Russian Twists

Chapter 7: Plyometric Exercises 89

    68 Double-Leg Spring (Forward and Backward)

    69 Single-Leg Hop (Forward and Backward)

    70 Forward Leg Springs With Chest Pass

    71 Double-Leg Spring Forward With an Over-the-Back Throw

    72 Double-Leg Spring Forward With an Underhand Forward Throw

    73 Overhead Backward Throw Off a Box

    74 Underhand Forward Throw Off a Box

    75 Over-the-Back Throw Off a Box

    76 Lateral Forward Jumps in Sand

    77 Forward-Forward-Back in Sand

    78 Counter Movement Jump

    79 Three-Step Vertical Jump

    80 Box Jump

    81 Drop Jumps

Chapter 8: Drills With Hurdles 99

    82 Continuous Stepovers

    83 Lateral Stepovers

- **84** Hurdle Taps
- **85** Takeoffs Over a Hurdle
- **86** Hurdle Hamstring Massage
- **87** Hamstring Stretch on a Hurdle
- **88** Pop Offs Over Barriers

Chapter 9: Drills With Balance Apparatus ... 107

- **89** Around the Worlds
- **90** Physioball March on Shoulders
- **91** Back Hypers on a Physioball
- **92** Balance on a Physioball
- **93** Balance on Knees With Toss
- **94** Lying on Back With Marching

Chapter 10: Supplemental Exercises ... 115

- **95** Side Walks
- **96** Forward Lateral Walks
- **97** Hamstring Curl
- **98** Piriformis Massage
- **99** Foot Massage With a Ball
- **100** Bridge
- **101** Barefoot Walks

References and Recommended Reading ... 122

About the Authors ... 124

Introduction

This book is written for serious athletes and coaches. Whether you are a high school or college-level coach, parent-coach, or trainer, the information provided in this text is a necessary companion for you to have in your reference materials.

The drills and exercises contained in this book have yielded proven results and have formed a basis for the many national champions and Olympians who have utilized these drills. The drills are presented in an easy to follow format that allows the reader to find drills pertinent to specific developmental phases of the high-jump event. And while this book is entitled 101 High Jump Drills, athletes from any sport or event that requires explosive movement, core strength, agility, and jumping ability can benefit from its use.

Cliff Rovelto's 33 years of experience coaching elite-class track and field athletes, along with my 18 years of experience competing as an elite-level athlete, has produced a timely, practical, hands-on book that will enhance your training program and provide results.

These drills can be used to enhance performance, taking into consideration the training age and abilities of your athletes. It is necessary to proceed slowly and understand that many of the exercises that seem quite simple are actually very difficult for even the best athletes to master. Exercises that are core-specific and involve balance can often tax the neuromuscular system more than you might imagine. The recommended repetitions included for each drill are average numbers; they can be decreased to meet the abilities of your athlete. References to recommended readings on periodization of training and other more in-depth materials are listed at the end of this book. The sky is the limit!

—Gwen Wentland

1

Warm-Up Drills

A warm-up is an essential part of any physical activity. The warm-up phase gives the neuromuscular system an opportunity to become activated and to prepare for the work ahead. Each drill explained in this chapter can be used as a warm-up for any of the jumping events, but is specifically tailored to developing the coordination, agility, and strength that are essential to the high jump. These drills can be done all together for a general warm-up routine or may be combined with short jogging and sprinting in between each drill to form a dynamic warm-up routine. A length of 20 to 30 meters is an appropriate distance for each drill. The emphasis should be on technical quality rather than quantity of repetitions or distance. Following is an example of an event-specific warm-up routine.

High Jump Continuous Warm-Up Routine

- Jog (100m)
- Side shuffle (100m)
- Jog (100m)
- Carioca (50m on each side)
- Jog (100m)
- Backward run (50m)
- Walk with arm circles, shoulder rotations (50m)
- Stride with arm rotations (forward and backward) (100m)
- Head circles, trunk rotation, hip circles, lower leg circles, ankle rotations (10 reps each)
- Zombies (50m)
- Speed skaters (10 reps)

- Soleus and gastroc stretch on wall
- Walk on heels with varying foot positions (toes inward, outward, inversion, eversion)
- Scorpion and iron cross (10 reps each)
- Low step and scoop as you go (50m)
- Leg swings front and side (10 reps each)
- Ankle pops (20m)
- Butt kicks (20m)
- Straight leg bounds tripling with fast leg cycle (20m on each leg)
- "A" skip (20m)
- "B" skip (20m)
- "A" run tripling with fast leg cycle (30m on each leg)
- Egg shells (20m)
- Sewing machine (20m)
- Walking lunges (20m)
- Running A (2 x 60m)
- Skipping takeoff (2 x 60m)
- Stride rhythm runs (4 x 10)
- Continuous circles (3 reps in each direction)
- Figure 8 (4 reps)
- Continuous circles with pop-offs (2 reps in each direction)
- Continuous pop-offs (2 x 60m)
- Acceleration on curve (3 x 60m, once each at 70%, 80%, and 90%)

Drill #1: Prisoner Squats

Objective: To improve quadricep and gluteus strength

Equipment Needed: None

Description: The athlete starts with his legs shoulder-width apart and his arms out in front. He squats down and holds for 30 seconds. Three to five repetitions of 20 to 30 seconds each are recommended.

Coaching Points: Look for the athlete to squat down to 90 degrees. Make sure the athlete does not allow the knee to extend out over the ankle joint, since that position would put too much pressure on the patellar tendon.

Drill #2: Zombies

Objective: To stretch the hamstring muscles; to warm up the hip flexors

Equipment Needed: None

Description: While walking, the athlete kicks his left leg as high as possible, touching the left toe with the right hand. On the next step, he kicks his right leg as high as possible, touching the right toe with the left hand. These kicks can be done for 20 to 40 meters.

Coaching Point: Look for the athlete to kick out with full extension.

Drill #3: Walking With Varying Foot Positions

Objective: To stretch the supportive tendons of the foot and ankle; to increase overall foot strength

Equipment Needed: None

Description: The athlete walks with varying foot positions (i.e., inversion, eversion, toes in, toes out). This drill can be done in bare feet or with shoes on. The recommended distance for this drill is 20 to 40 meters.

Coaching Point: This drill should be done on grass if possible.

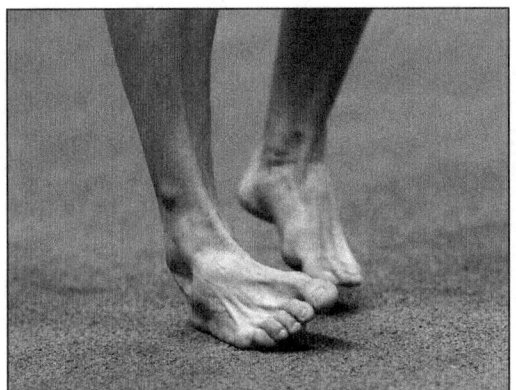
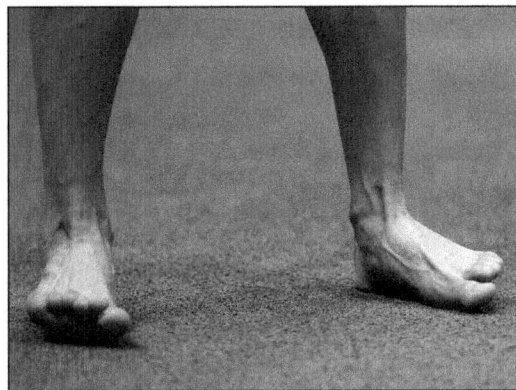
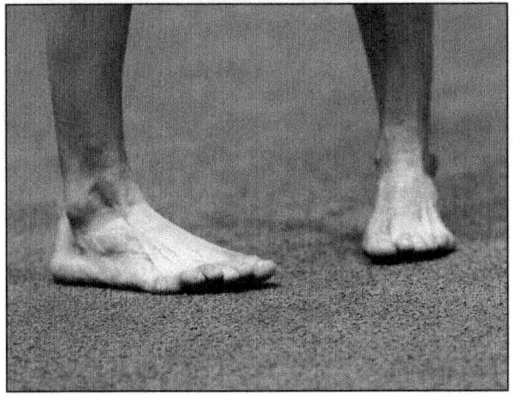
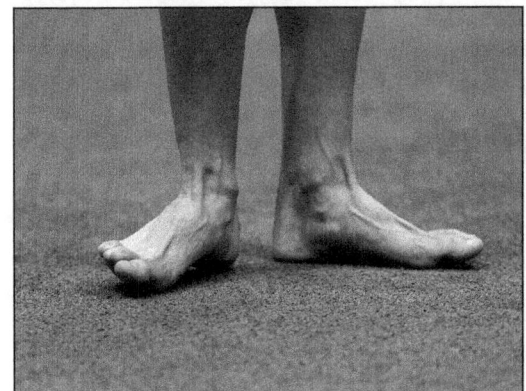

Drill #4: Speed Skaters

Objective: To strengthen and stretch the legs, specifically the quadriceps

Equipment Needed: None

Description: The athlete starts in a standing position, with his feet shoulder-width apart. He hops to the left, taking the right leg and crossing it behind the left leg, like a speed skater. The arms follow in the direction of the legs. The athlete then hops to the right, and continues going from one side to another for 10 repetitions.

Coaching Points: Look for the athlete to stretch the back leg behind the front leg. He should be moving in a continuous side-to-side pattern.

Drill #5: Iron Cross

Objective: To develop back and hip flexibility

Equipment Needed: None

Description: The athlete lies on his back with his arms out like a cross. He takes his right leg up to meet his left hand, brings the leg back to the starting position, and performs the same movement from the opposite side. Ten repetitions to each side are recommended.

Coaching Points: Make sure the athlete keeps his leg low when crossing it over the body. He should maintain dorsiflexion in the foot of the leg that is extended on the ground and attempt to keep the toes directed toward the sky throughout the movement.

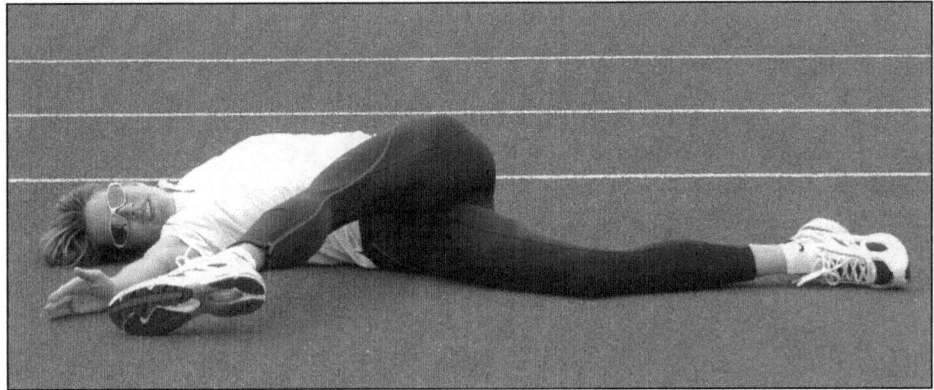

Drill #6: Scorpion

Objective: To increase back and hip flexibility

Equipment Needed: None

Description: The athlete lies on his stomach with his arms out like a cross. He swings his left leg up to meet his right hand, brings the leg back down to the starting position, and performs the same movement from the opposite side. Ten repetitions to each side are recommended.

Coaching Point: Make sure the athlete keeps his leg low when crossing it over the body.

Drill #7: Egg Shells

Objective: To stimulate the neuromuscular system; to encourage foot quickness

Equipment Needed: None

Description: The athlete performs a quick shuffle on his toes, like he is crushing egg shells beneath his feet. The athlete should jog a few steps, then "crush the shells" for five to six quick steps. This activity can be done for 20 to 30 meters.

Coaching Points: The athlete should perform this drill with a slight bend in the knees. This drill can be used in conjunction with a dynamic warm-up routine.

Drill #8: Sewing Machine

Objective: To stimulate the neuromuscular system; to strengthen the core and hips

Equipment Needed: None

Description: Maintaining an erect posture, the athlete brings his knees up high and quick, like the needle of a sewing machine, keeping his toes in a dorsiflexed (upward) position. The athlete should jog a few steps, then do the needle action for five to six quick steps, and so on, for 20 to 30 meters.

Coaching Point: Make sure the athlete's foot maintains a dorsiflexed position.

Drill #9: Forward Low Walks

Objective: To strengthen the legs and hips in a low body position

Equipment Needed: None

Description: The athlete assumes a squatting position and walks forward, taking elongated steps in a "hips low" position, with his arms behind his back, for 20 to 40 meters.

Coaching Points: See that the athlete's hips stay in a low position and his ankle stays out in front of the knee joint.

Drill #10: Running A

Objective: To develop hip strength; to encourage good running form

Equipment Needed: None

Description: The athlete runs forward, keeping the knees high and keeping the feet in a dorsiflexed position. He concentrates on working into the ground as opposed to landing on the ground and then working. The recommended distance for this drill is 20 to 40 meters.

Coaching Points: See that the athlete maintains erect posture and proper foot position. He should keep the foot dorsiflexed and step over the opposite leg.

Drill #11: Leg Swings

Objective: To develop good hip flexibility and back mobility

Equipment Needed: None

Description: This drill is done in two positions. The first is with the athlete standing with his hands on a wall or railing for support, swinging his right leg across the body as high and as far out as possible. The second is with the athlete standing with a wall or railing at his right side for support, swinging his right leg as high as possible to the front and rear. He should perform 10 repetitions in each position, then switch to the opposite leg.

Drill #12: Pretzel Glute Stretch

Objective: To stretch the gluteus muscles

Equipment Needed: None

Description: Sitting on the ground with both legs straight out in front, the athlete crosses one leg over the other. He wraps his arms around the bent leg, stretching the gluteus muscles. He should hold the stretch for 10 seconds, then switch legs.

Coaching Point: This drill is good to include in a warm-up or warm-down sequence.

Drill #13: Dribble With Roundhouse Karate Kick

Objective: To develop hip mobility

Equipment Needed: None

Description: The athlete takes approximately five small jogging steps into a high karate kick, repeating the jog-kick combination with one leg for 30 meters. Then, he performs the drill with the other leg for 30 meters.

Coaching Point: The athlete should concentrate on bringing the kicking leg as high into the air as possible.

2

Approach Drills

The most important element of the high-jump approach is the beginning. A smooth, consistent, fast, and reasonably tight radius will lead to successful jumping. Most high-jump literature calls for a 10-step approach, initiating the curve in the transition of steps five and six.

A large amount of time should be spent developing and perfecting the approach. The drills in this chapter can be done alone or in combination with high-jump practice. During the track season, you can include a number of these drills in practice, up to three times a week.

Drill #14: Ladder Accelerations

Objective: To increase coordination and foot quickness

Equipment Needed: A training ladder or pieces of tape

Description: Using a training ladder or tape, set markers at distances of 40cm, 50cm, and 60cm, and in increments of 10cm thereafter. The athlete accelerates by pushing back against the ground and sprinting off the end of the ladder pattern. An appropriate setup would be six to eight marks with a 10-meter runoff. Five to ten repetitions are recommended.

Coaching Point: The athlete must learn to overcome inertia by pushing out of the back when beginning his high-jump approach.

Drill #15: Acceleration Using Resistance

Objective: To develop good sprinting form and knee lift

Equipment Needed: A harness, a wall, or a weighted vest

Description: If using a wall, the athlete places both hands on the wall with the body at an angle of approximately 45 degrees. The athlete runs, lifting his knees for 5 to 10 seconds or 5 to 10 repetitions. By doing so, the athlete learns to apply force by pushing with resistance. If using a harness or a weighted vest, the athlete runs on the track for 20 to 30 meters focusing on pushing mechanics.

Coaching Point: Look for acute shin angles with the ground and complete extension of the hips.

Drill #16: Approaches With Hand Weights

Objective: To help the athlete learn to engage the arms and conceptualize the approach in slow motion

Equipment Needed: Small hand weights weighing less than five pounds

Description: The athlete walks through his approach while holding the hand weights, concentrating on correct arm movements. Five repetitions of the approach are recommended.

Coaching Points: The arm swing should come from the shoulder, and the torso should not lean separate from the lower body. This drill could be inserted into a warm-up or warm-down routine.

Drill #17: Rhythm Runs

Objective: To acquaint the athlete with the feeling of building speed throughout the full approach

Equipment Needed: None

Description: The athlete counts to himself while running 10 steps forward without curving. The counting pattern should be 1-2-3, 1-2-3, 1-2-3, hit. The rhythm should be from slow to fast. This drill can be done for six to eight repetitions.

Coaching Points: The last two steps should be quick. The athlete should hit and keep heel recovery low.

Drill #18: Curve Running

Objective: To simulate the feeling of proper body lean caused by a tight and fast high-jump approach

Equipment Needed: Track curve

Description: The athlete sprints around the curve of the track, emphasizing proper curve-running mechanics for 30 to 60 meters. The turnover should be quick, and the foot should be dorsiflexed. The shoulder that would be closest to the high-jump bar during the jump should be kept back; it should not come forward of the body. The shoulder should be on the same plane as the hips.

Coaching Point: Make sure the athlete maintains an erect posture, with his shoulders in correct alignment with his hips.

Drill #19: Circles

Objective: To simulate the feeling of proper body lean caused by a tight and fast high-jump approach

Equipment Needed: A large area that is free of obstacles, or a high-jump apron

Description: The athlete runs in a circle with sufficient speed to create pressure against the ground, resulting in a lean to the inside of the circle. The radius of the circle should be tight enough to encourage inward body lean. The lean originates at the ankle, creating pressure against the ground.

Coaching Points: Make sure the athlete keeps good posture and running mechanics. The athlete must push his inside leg to the midline of his body to maintain pressure. This drill should be done in both directions to maintain muscle balance. The radius of the athlete's high-jump approach can be calculated and used for this drill. The length of the radius is determined by the coach's observation of running mechanics and the athlete's ability to maintain proper postural positions.

Drill #20: Figure Eights

Objective: To teach the athlete what it feels like to put pressure against the ground and run a curve that creates lean

Equipment Needed: A large area that is free of obstacles, or a high-jump apron

Description: The athlete runs in a figure eight pattern, forcing him to run in both directions on the curve. The athlete should feel the transition of lean as he changes directions. Three to four repetitions are recommended.

Coaching Points: Make sure the athlete accelerates into and out of the curve to maintain pressure, and that he relaxes on the straight portion of the figure eight. Look for acute shin angles when the athlete is in the curve.

Drill #21: Approaches on the High-Jump Apron

Objective: To allow the athlete to work on the rhythm of the high-jump approach without the stress of jumping

Equipment Needed: None

Description: The athlete runs his approaches on the apron without actually executing a jump. Five to eight repetitions are recommended.

Coaching Points: The athlete should run by the pit, continuing on around as if he were running a circle. This action enables the athlete to maintain pressure against the ground throughout the approach.

Drill #22: Assisted Sprints

Objective: To increase turnover when sprinting

Equipment Needed: A bungee cord, a decline, a pulling system, or the wind

Description: The athlete sprints with assistance, i.e. on a decline, using a bungee cord or pulling system, or with the wind. Three to five repetitions of 20 to 30 meters are recommended.

Coaching Points: This drill is a very effective special strength exercise that provides contrast in breaking speed barriers. Make sure the athlete does not resist the assistance. He should relax and let gravity or the equipment pull him.

Drill #23: "S" Runs

Objective: To simulate foot pressure associated with the curved portion of the high-jump approach

Equipment Needed: None

Description: The athlete runs on the straightaway, sweeping from side to side in a serpentine pattern. Five repetitions of 80 to 100 meters are recommended.

Coaching Points: See that the athlete runs enough of an "S" to create body lean and foot pressure analogous to running a curve in the high jump. The athlete's foot position should be toes up.

3

Takeoff Mechanism Drills

The objective in the high-jump takeoff is to convert horizontal velocity into vertical velocity. At takeoff, the athlete should apply a large force quickly, through as great a range of motion as possible. To accomplish this task, the athlete needs to move over the penultimate (next-to-last) step and do so in as low a position as his strength level will allow, while maintaining an erect posture. The takeoff leg is fired into the ground using the gluteus and hamstring muscles. The quadriceps contract eccentrically to stabilize the takeoff leg, keeping knee flexion to a minimum. The last two foot contacts should be flat, with the takeoff foot brought through low to the ground.

Drill #24: Circles With Pop Offs

Objective: To improve curve running; to recreate the sensation of moving over the penultimate foot; to teach rhythm and coordination skills

Equipment Needed: A large area that is free of obstacles, or a high-jump apron

Description: The athlete pops off every sixth step while running in a circle. When running in the counterclockwise direction, the athlete pops off the left leg and lands on the right leg, continuing to run in a circle. The exact opposite is executed when traveling in a clockwise direction. Three to six circle repetitions with pop offs are recommended.

Coaching Points: Make sure the athlete focuses on moving horizontally as opposed to vertically when popping off. The athlete should emphasize quick, fast, and flat contacts on the last two steps.

Drill #25: Long-Jump Takeoffs

Objective: To develop a quick penultimate step

Equipment Needed: High-jump pit or long-jump pit

Description: The athlete performs a short approach of four to six steps and executes a long jump into sand or onto the top of the high-jump mats. Five to ten repetitions are recommended.

Coaching Points: The athlete's hips should be moving over the penultimate foot. The last two foot contacts should be flat.

Drill #26: Pop Offs Over Low Barriers

Objective: To develop quickness and overall agility

Equipment Needed: Short hurdles or hurdles that have been flipped upside down

Description: The athlete pops off over 5 to 10 barriers placed six to eight feet apart, making two quick contacts in between hurdles. The barrier height should be set at 12 to 18 inches for women and 18 to 24 inches for men. Three repetitions are recommended.

Coaching Point: See that the athlete has quick, flat-footed contacts.

Drill #27: Hurdling

Objective: To teach rhythm and the takeoff mechanism

Equipment Needed: Four to five hurdles

Description: The athlete hurdles over four to five barriers. This drill can be performed using three or five steps in between the hurdles. If using three steps in between hurdles, the recommended spacing is 7.0 to 8.5 meters for women and 8.5 to 9.14 meters for men. If using five steps in between hurdles, the recommended spacing is 11 to 12 meters for women and 12 to 13 meters for men. Three to six sets of four to five hurdles is recommended.

Coaching Point: The height of the barrier should be kept low enough for the athlete to get over it comfortably.

Drill #28: Gallop

Objective: To recreate the push-pull sensation associated with the takeoff mechanism

Equipment Needed: None

Description: The athlete pushes off his back leg with good extension of the hip while firing the front leg down into the ground in a dorsiflexed (toe up) position. Three repetitions with a distance of 40 meters are recommended.

Coaching Points: This drill aids in teaching the takeoff mechanism. The athlete's motion should look similar to what a child looks like when riding a wooden stick horse.

Drill #29: Oliver Drill* With Hurdles

Objective: To strengthen the penultimate step

Equipment Needed: Two hurdles

Description: The athlete places the penultimate foot forward, maintaining an erect posture, then pushes his hips through and over the penultimate foot. The athlete moves forward and backward over the penultimate foot while leaving it in place. Three sets of 10 repetitions are recommended.

Coaching Points: This drill is good for introductory takeoff practice. The athlete's lead knee should be moving toward the ground, and his hips should be pushing through on a level plane.

*This exercise was originally devised by Arturo Oliver and is included in Gordon, B. & Dapena, J. (1999). *Women's High Jump #19. Scientific Services* Project. USA Track & Field. Biomechanics Laboratory, Dept. of Kinesiology, Indiana University.

Drill #30: Oliver Drill* With One Step

Objective: To strengthen the hips in a low-body position for takeoff

Equipment Needed: A weighted bar (optional)

Description: The athlete starts in a static position. Then, the athlete pushes off gently with the back leg (the takeoff leg), to place the weight of the body over the non-takeoff leg. The body then slowly passes over the non-takeoff leg, and, finally, the takeoff leg is placed ahead on the ground to stop the forward motion. After stopping for an instant, the athlete makes a slight push forward on the ground with his takeoff leg, forcing him backward into the original starting position. The exercise should be repeated for three sets of 10 repetitions or until the non-takeoff leg becomes tired.

Coaching Points: See that the athlete is moving over the non-takeoff foot in a low position. A weighted bar can be added as the athlete gains more control with the exercise.

*This exercise was originally devised by Arturo Oliver and is included in Gordon, B. & Dapena, J. (1999). *Women's High Jump #19. Scientific Services* Project. USA Track & Field. Biomechanics Laboratory, Dept. of Kinesiology, Indiana University.

Drill #31: Oliver Drill* With Three Steps

Objective: To teach the athlete to keep his hips low in the penultimate step and to "catch his hips on the rise" at takeoff

Equipment Needed: A weighted bar (optional)

Description: Beginning with the takeoff foot forward, the athlete steps forward and continues to move forward over the penultimate foot (while lowering his hips), and then executes a footstrike with the takeoff foot. Three sets of 10 repetitions are recommended.

Coaching Points: See that the athlete's hips stay low and do not rise up as the takeoff foot comes forward. A weighted bar can be added as the athlete gains more control with the exercise.

*This exercise was originally devised by Arturo Oliver and is included in Gordon, B. & Dapena, J. (1999). *Women's High Jump #19*. Scientific Services Project. USA Track & Field. Biomechanics Laboratory, Dept. of Kinesiology, Indiana University.

Drill #32: One-Box Penultimate

Objective: To provide the athlete the sensation of compressing on the penultimate leg

Equipment Needed: A box (four inches high)

Description: The athlete stands on his takeoff leg at the end and side of the box. The athlete then steps forward, placing the penultimate leg on the ground. This contact should be flat and the athlete should move over this flat-foot contact, placing the takeoff leg back on the box and extending the takeoff leg as would be desired in a takeoff.

Coaching Points: The feet should remain dorsiflexed and the athlete should make full foot contact with the ground on the penultimate and takeoff strides. The athlete should strive to make contact with the ground with the foot beneath the hips.

Drill #33: Box-Ground-Box Long Jump Takeoffs With Run-Up

Objective: To provide the athlete the sensation of compressing on the penultimate leg

Equipment Needed: Two boxes with six to eight feet between the boxes (The distance between the boxes will depend on the length of the run-up—the longer the run-up, the greater the distance between boxes.)

Description: Using a run-up of four or more steps, the athlete approaches, placing the takeoff leg on the first box, then the penultimate leg on the ground, and then the takeoff leg on the second box. The athlete is simply doing a four-step (or more) long jump takeoff drill with the boxes spaced out in such a way that the takeoff foot will land on the boxes and the penultimate leg will be on the ground.

Coaching Points: The run-up increases the loading of the penultimate leg and provides the athlete the sensation of moving over the compressed penultimate leg. Primary emphasis is on executing a proper penultimate step. The athlete should move over the compressed penultimate leg with speed. Takeoff itself is a long jump takeoff, not a high jump takeoff—the athlete should perform this drill on a long jump runway and land in the sand for safety.

Drill #34: Skipping Takeoffs

Objective: To develop rhythm and strength necessary for takeoff

Equipment Needed: A weighted bar (optional)

Description: The athlete skips down the track, executing a high-jump takeoff every other step. Three repetitions with a distance of 30 to 40 meters is recommended.

Coaching Points: The takeoff leg should be straight when fired into the ground. The athlete should keep his foot dorsiflexed and the plant flat-footed. He should take off and land on the same leg. A weighted bar can be used as the athlete gains more experience with the drill.

Drill #35: Standing Takeoffs With Spot

Objective: To aid with proper takeoff position keeping the shoulder closest to the bar back; to keep the athlete's body position from leaning into the bar upon takeoff

Equipment Needed: A spotter

Description: The athlete performs a takeoff drill from a standing position, with the penultimate foot forward. As the athlete has no momentum, he should actually fall backward. A coach or teammate should stand to the side of the athlete performing the drill and spot him as he falls backward. Three sets of five repetitions are recommended.

Coaching Points: The spotter must be ready. The athlete executing the takeoff must feel confident that they will be caught.

Drill #36: Three-Step Takeoffs

Objective: To aid with proper takeoff position keeping the shoulder closest to the bar back; to keep the athlete's body position from leaning into the bar upon takeoff

Equipment Needed: A spotter, a weighted bar

Description: The athlete executes a takeoff drill, adding three steps to create *momentum*. Three sets of 10 repetitions are recommended.

Coaching Points: The athlete performing the takeoff drill should still fall backward, as there will not be sufficient centrifugal force to carry the athlete into the pit if she was jumping vertically. A weighted bar can be added as the athlete gains more experience.

Drill #37: Scissors

Objective: To strengthen the hips and free-leg drive

Equipment Needed: A high-jump apron, a pit

Description: The athlete runs his approach, executing a scissor jump at the takeoff point, taking him into the pit. The athlete should land on his feet in the pit. Five to ten scissor jumps are recommended.

Coaching Point: The athlete must grab the ground on the penultimate step, move over it, and get off the step quickly.

Drill #38: High Jump Off an Elevated Surface

Objective: To help the athlete with timing over higher barriers; to allow the athlete to visualize higher bar heights

Equipment Needed: A high-jump apron, a pit

Description: The athlete executes a high jump from a raised surface in the form of a raised box or ramp. Eight to ten jumps are recommended.

Coaching Points: This drill is excellent for takeoff and bar clearance work because by raising the takeoff surface, the athlete can execute an effective takeoff with more ease. This exercise also allows the athlete to work on timing his jump over the top of the bar at higher heights.

4

Bar-Clearance Drills

Quite simply, the athlete, upon leaving the ground at takeoff, must rotate about the crossbar. One of the reasons the high jumper runs on a curve or portion of a circle is to create centrifugal force, which carries the athlete into the pit. The athlete must feel comfortable landing high on his back. For this reason, utilizing drills that will build the athlete's confidence in this aspect is important, and particularly necessary for a beginner. The drills in this chapter focus on improving bar clearance and landing technique. It should be noted, however, that these techniques should not be overemphasized when teaching the high jump. The rotation about the bar is primarily a function of running a good curve and executing an effective takeoff.

Drill #39: Back Overs

Objective: To teach the athlete to look back; to create the feeling of arching

Equipment Needed: A high-jump pit

Description: The athlete stands on the pit and performs a backflip, landing on his stomach. Ten repetitions of this drill are recommended.

Coaching Points: Make sure the athlete becomes comfortable performing this drill. It may be helpful to use a spotter on the first few attempts.

Drill #40: Back Overs Off the Ground

Objective: To create the sensation of moving up and over the high-jump bar and landing high on the shoulders

Equipment Needed: A high-jump pit

Description: The athlete stands approximately arm's-length away from the bar, with his back facing the bar and pit. He then jumps up and back over the bar. Ten jumps over the bar are recommended.

Coaching Points: The athlete should land high on his shoulders and roll over. This drill works well for beginners.

Drill #41: Back Overs Off a Box

Objective: To improve bar clearance and timing from an elevated surface

Equipment Needed: A high-jump pit, a box (12 to 18 inches high)

Description: The athlete stands on the box, approximately arm's-length away from the bar, with his back facing the bar and pit. He then jumps up and back over the bar. Ten jumps over the bar are recommended.

Coaching Points: Jumping off the box gives the athlete more air time, thereby assisting him with the timing over the bar.

Drill #42: Run Up Off Two Feet

Objective: To train the athlete to time up his rotation with increased horizontal momentum

Equipment Needed: A high-jump pit

Description: Taking three to four running steps straight at the bar, the athlete comes to a jump stop in front of the bar while turning his back to the bar. He then jumps backward over the bar, landing on his shoulders. Five to eight jumps are recommended.

Coaching Points: This drill adds momentum to the back-over drill and can be used more effectively following the comprehension of back overs.

Drill #43: Wrestler's Arch

Objective: To assist and increase back strength and abdominal flexibility

Equipment Needed: None

Description: The athlete lies on his back and places his arms overhead with his palms on the ground. The athlete arches up into a bridge position and holds for two to three seconds. Ten repetitions are recommended.

Coaching Point: Back support may be needed if the athlete has trouble getting into this position.

5

Special Strength Exercises

Special strength drills are intended to build strength in muscles that are event-specific. Following this section is a list of exercises essential to the high jumper's needs. The drills in this chapter focus on developing core body strength, flexibility through a dynamic range of motion, and kinesthetic awareness of the body.

Using his own body weight, in conjunction with medicine balls and physioballs, an athlete can develop effective special strength circuits that can be used year-round. Whether you are working with an amateur or an elite-level athlete, these exercises will enhance overall athleticism. These drills can be customized to match the athlete's strength level and training age. Due to this variable, the repetitions for several of the medicine-ball exercises will need to be adjusted accordingly.

An emphasis should be placed on improving the core strength of the athlete. The benefits of improving core or pillar body strength include resistance to injury, improved posture, and improved force-production capability. In addition to traditional sit-ups, drills that include balance and back strength are essential to creating a stable core. Following is an example of a core routine.

Core Routine

- Hanging knee-ups (20 reps)
- Wheelbarrow (forward and backward) (10m)
- Side-ups (15 reps on each side)
- Walking lunge with stretch (10 reps)
- Backward walks (10m)
- L-ups with push (10 reps)

- Diagonals (bottom to top with 5-second count, 5 reps each side) (use medicine ball for resistance)
- Diagonals (top to bottom with 5-second count, 5 reps each side) (use medicine ball for resistance)
- Diagonals (bottom to top with throw, 5 reps each side) (use medicine ball for resistance)
- Walking lunge with medicine ball held overhead (10m)
- Marching A with medicine ball held overhead (10m)

Drill #44: Wheelbarrow

Objective: To improve core body strength, along with arm and shoulder strength

Equipment Needed: A partner

Description: A partner holds the athlete's legs while the athlete walks on his hands forward and backward for 10 steps in each direction.

Coaching Point: See that the athlete does not drop his hips.

Drill #45: Side-Ups

Objective: To strengthen the oblique muscles

Equipment Needed: An elevated surface, a partner

Description: A partner holds down the athlete's legs as the athlete leans at the hips off an elevated surface, such as a table. While lying on his side, the athlete performs side-ups to just above parallel to the hips. Three sets of 15 repetitions are recommended.

Coaching Points: It is important to go through the entire range of motion, up and down. After the athlete gains some strength, weight can be added to this drill by having the athlete hold a weight to his chest or hold smaller weights with his arms extended.

Drill #46: L-Ups With Push

Objective: To strengthen the lower abdominals and hip muscles

Equipment Needed: A partner

Description: The athlete holds onto his partner's ankles while lying in the supine position. He raises his feet over his head, and the partner then pushes the athlete's legs toward the ground in varying directions. The athlete resists the pushing and brings his legs back up before they touch the ground. Two sets of 10 to 20 repetitions are recommended.

Coaching Point: See that the athlete's legs are straight and that his legs do not touch the ground.

Drill #47: Diagonals

Objective: To develop abdominal and back strength; to develop overall flexibility

Equipment Needed: A medicine ball

Description: The athlete begins by holding a medicine ball with his arms extended overhead and slanted over his right shoulder. He moves the ball in an arc from that position toward the ground, to a position just outside the left foot. Ten repetitions are recommended. After performing a complete set from upper right to lower left, the athlete should switch sides and perform a set of 10 repetitions from upper left to lower right.

Coaching Point: Make sure the athlete's movement stays slow and controlled.

Drill #48: Partner Exchange With Toss

Objective: To develop midsection flexibility and strength

Equipment Needed: A medicine ball, a partner

Description: The athlete and his partner stand about two feet apart, with their backs toward each other. The person with the ball stretches back to his right and hands the ball to the other person who is stretched back to his right, exchanging the ball as they come to the center. This action creates a smooth stretching motion for the torso. Ten repetitions to both sides are recommended.

Coaching Point: The athlete should focus on developing low back and torso flexibility. When the coach is assisting the athlete he should stand behind him and hold the ball as the athlete exchanges if from side to side.

Drill #49: Hanging Russian Hamstring

Objective: To increase hamstring strength

Equipment Needed: A pull-up bar, a partner

Description: The athlete hangs from the pull-up bar while his partner stands about three feet away facing him. The athlete puts his left leg on the partner's shoulder and pushes down on the shoulder while driving the hips upward. Ten repetitions using each leg are recommended.

Coaching Point: The athlete should concentrate on driving his heel into the shoulder of the partner to isolate the hamstring muscle.

Drill #50: Hanging Knee Raises With Medicine Ball

Objective: To develop core and hip strength

Equipment Needed: Pull-up bar, a medicine ball

Description: The athlete places a medicine ball between his knees and holds onto a pull-up bar. The athlete brings his knees to his chest and back down in a controlled manner. Three sets of 10 repetitions are recommended.

Coaching Points: Do not allow the athlete to swing back and forth. As the athlete becomes stronger, heavier medicine balls can be used with this exercise.

6

More Exercises With Weight

Adding weight to drills can be an effective means to strengthen event-specific muscle groups and enhance proper muscle-order firing. This chapter includes drills using weighted bars, medicine balls, or shot puts, along with drills using partner resistance.

The drills using medicine balls and/or shot puts can be combined to form multiple-throw routines. The recommended weight used in these drills is 6.6 to 8.8 pounds for women, and 12 to 16 pounds for men. Other drills mentioned in this chapter utilize a weighted bar. These drills can be implemented into daily workout routines or as part of a special strength program. Following is an example of a multiple-throw routine.

Multiple-Throw Routine #1 (Using a Medicine Ball or Shot Put)

- Overhead backward throw (5 reps)
- Underhand forward throw (5 reps)
- Hay toss left (5 reps)
- Hay toss right (5 reps)
- Chest pass (5 reps)

Drill #51: Overhead Backward Throw

Objective: To develop explosive strength in the legs

Equipment Needed: A medicine ball or shot put

Description: The athlete starts in a standing position with the medicine ball (or shot put) overhead. The athlete squats down to an angle of 90 degrees, then explodes upward and releases the weight overhead. Five to ten throws are recommended.

Coaching Points: See that the athlete is using his hips to initiate the movement. Make sure he is not bending forward at the waist when bringing the ball down.

Drill #52: Underhand Forward Throw

Objective: To develop explosive strength in the legs

Equipment Needed: A medicine ball or shot put

Description: The athlete starts in a standing position with the medicine ball (or shot put) overhead. The athlete lowers the weight between his legs and concurrently squats down, followed by a powerful extension of the hips and an underhand throw forward. Five to ten throws are recommended.

Coaching Points: See that the athlete is using his hips to initiate the movement. Make sure he is not bending forward at the waist when bringing the ball down. The explosion should take the athlete forward following the throwexplosion should take the athlete forward following the throw.

Drill #53: Hay Toss Left and Right

Objective: To increase range of motion; to strengthen the obliques

Equipment Needed: A medicine ball or shot put

Description: The athlete holds the medicine ball (or shot put) on one side of his body, just below the hip, then brings the weight up and releases it over his opposite shoulder. Five to ten throws to each side of the body are recommended.

Coaching Point: This drill is a very effective core exercise.

Drill #54: Arms—Single Support

Objective: To strengthen the arms and shoulders

Equipment Needed: Light hand weights weighing less than three pounds

Description: While holding hand weights, the athlete stands on one leg and executes the arm movements utilized in takeoff. Thirty seconds of arm action are recommended.

Coaching Point: This drill could be utilized as part of a strength routine.

Drill #55: Arms—Double Support

Objective: To strengthen arm drive motion

Equipment Needed: Hand weights weighing three to five pounds

Description: While holding hand weights, the athlete stands on both legs and executes the arm movements utilized in takeoff. The double support enables the athlete to use more weight and to emphasize more of the blocking action. Ten to twenty seconds of arm action are recommended.

Coaching Point: This drill could be utilized as part of a strength routine.

Drill #56: Arms—Physioball

Objective: To work shoulder strength and emphasize arm action with core balance at the same time

Equipment Needed: A physioball, hand weights weighing three to five pounds

Description: Using a physioball, the athlete balances on his knees atop the ball with hand weights in each hand. He takes his arms back and drives them to an arm block, stopping at eye level. Three sets of 10 repetitions are recommended.

Coaching Point: Have beginners focus on balancing atop the ball first, finding their center of gravity, then add the arm block.

Drill #57: Curve Running

Objective: To simulate the high-jump curve with a focus on shoulder position and with weight resistance

Equipment Needed: A stick or weighted bar

Description: The athlete runs on the curve of the track holding a stick or weighted bar on his shoulders. Four repetitions running a distance of 60 to 100 meters are recommended.

Coaching Point: The bar encourages the athlete to remain erect and keep his shoulders perpendicular to the direction of run.

Drill #58: Walking Lunges

Objective: To strengthen hamstrings; to improve posture

Equipment Needed: A medicine ball or weighted bar

Description: The athlete performs alternating lunges with weight on his shoulders or held overhead for a distance of 20 to 40 meters.

Coaching Points: Pay special attention to the athlete's shin angle while lunging. The knee should not be in front of the ankle joint. This motion could put too much pressure on the patellar tendon, especially when lunging with heavy weight.

Drill #59: Takeoffs

Objective: To teach the correct order of firing for various muscle groups

Equipment Needed: A weighted bar, a box (four to six inches high)

Description: With weight on his shoulders, the athlete steps up onto a four- to six-inch box, pulling the takeoff foot back into the ground in a clawing motion. He then continues to follow through with his free leg. Three sets of 8 to 10 repetitions are recommended.

Coaching Point: The athlete's freeside hip should come through as a result of him firing his takeoff foot back into the box.

Drill #60: Leg Toss

Objective: To strengthen the hip flexors

Equipment Needed: A medicine ball

Description: The athlete places a medicine ball between his legs, holding it just above his ankles. He then jumps up and tosses the medicine ball forward. Three sets of 10 repetitions each are recommended.

Coaching Point: Make sure the medicine ball is the appropriate weight for the athlete.

Drill #61: Hamstring Curls

Objective: To develop hamstring strength

Equipment Needed: A medicine ball, a partner

Description: The athlete lies prone on the ground. The partner stands over the athlete's shoulders, facing his feet, and holding a medicine ball. The partner rolls the ball down the athlete's legs, starting at the gluteus. The athlete kicks up when the ball reaches near the ankles and tosses the ball back to the assistant. Three sets of 10 repetitions are recommended.

Coaching Points: Make sure the medicine ball is the appropriate weight for the athlete. The athlete on the ground must wait until the ball reaches his heels before firing the hamstrings.

Drill #62: Toss and Catch

Objective: To teach the athlete to both catch and throw using his hips

Equipment Needed: A medicine ball (8 to 12 pounds for women, 14 to 16 pounds for men)

Description: Holding the medicine ball at arm's-length away from the body, the athlete squats down to form a 90-degree angle and tosses the ball into the air, catching it on its return down. Three sets of 10 repetitions are recommended.

Coaching Points: The athlete should initiate the throw with his hips and absorb the weight of the ball on the descent. In other words, the athlete should catch the ball with his hips descending and throw the ball with his hips ascending. He should be thinking, "Catch and throw with my hips."

Drill #63: Walking Torso Twists

Objective: To build low-back and torso flexibility and hamstring strength

Equipment Needed: A medicine ball

Description: While performing a walking lunge, the athlete swings the medicine ball across his body toward the forward leg, twisting the torso. These lunges can be done for 30 meters.

Coaching Point: The athlete should be twisting with the ball across and over the front lunging leg.

Drill #64: Standing Knee Drive

Objective: To strengthen the hip flexors

Equipment Needed: A medicine ball, a wall or partner

Description: The athlete stands facing a wall or a partner. While in a split stance, the athlete places the medicine ball on the thigh of his rear leg and drives his knee upward, sending the ball toward the wall or partner. Three sets of 10 repetitions are recommended.

Coaching Points: The coach should cue the athlete to "fire hip" to emphasize that the force should come from driving the hip.

Drill #65: Back Hypers on a Bench With Toss

Objective: To strengthen the low back muscles

Equipment Needed: A medicine ball, two partners

Description: The athlete lies prone on a table, hanging off at the hips. One partner holds the athlete's legs, and the other tosses and catches the medicine ball with him. The athlete should catch the ball on the way up, go down with the ball, and return the throw when the torso reaches a horizontal position. Three sets of 10 repetitions are recommended.

Coaching Points: Make sure the medicine ball is the appropriate weight for the athlete. This exercise should be performed with control.

Drill #66: Seated Adductor Toss

Objective: To strengthen the adductor (inner thigh) muscle

Equipment Needed: A medicine ball

Description: The athlete sits on the ground with one leg out straight and the other leg pulled up into a figure-four position. The athlete then holds the medicine ball over the bent knee and drives through the ball by lifting his leg quickly. Three sets of 10 repetitions are recommended.

Coaching Point: Make sure the medicine ball is the appropriate weight for the athlete.

Drill #67: Seated Russian Twists

Objective: To improve abdominal strength

Equipment Needed: A medicine ball

Description: The athlete sits on the ground with his legs out straight and slightly raised off ground to isolate the abdominal muscles. The athlete then holds a medicine ball with his arms extended and brings the ball side to side across his body. Three sets of 10 repetitions are recommended.

Coaching Point: Make sure the athlete maintains an erect posture.

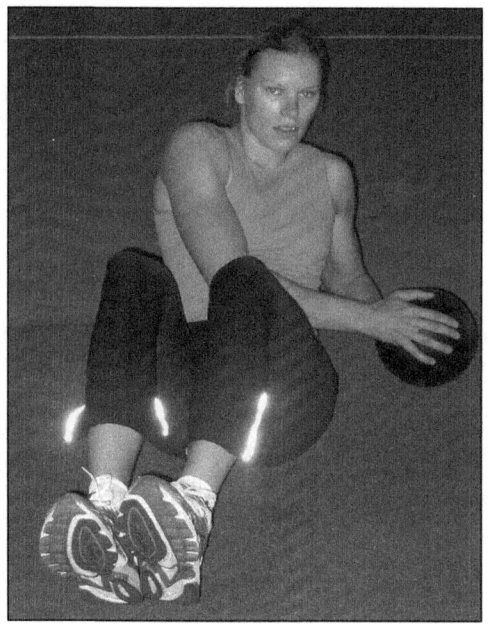

Plyometric Exercises

Plyometrics is a type of exercise training that enhances the elastic capabilities of the muscles and connective tissue. These exercises are characterized by eccentric loading, immediately followed by concentric movement. The plyometric drills mentioned in this chapter can be done for a distance of 10 to 30 meters. Following is an example of a plyometric progression routine that could be prescribed as part of a workout.

Plyometric Progression Routine

- Skip for height
- Skip for distance
- Double-leg spring (forward and backward)
- Single-leg hop (forward and backward)
- Speed bounds
- Gallop

Drill #68: Double-Leg Spring
(Forward and Backward)

Objective: To teach quality ground contact and the ability to apply force quickly

Equipment Needed: None

Description: The athlete springs forward with both legs for 20 to 30 meters firing from the hips, similar to moving on a pogo stick. The athlete's feet should be flat on contact, and he should apply force quickly, spending as little time on the ground as possible. The drill should then be done springing backward over the same distance. Two to three repetitions with a distance of 30 meters are recommended.

Coaching Point: The athlete should focus on the quality of his response with the ground as opposed to the magnitude of horizontal displacement.

Drill #69: Single-Leg Hop
(Forward and Backward)

Objective: To teach quality ground contact and the ability to apply force quickly

Equipment Needed: None

Description: The athlete hops forward on one leg for 10 to 30 meters, then hops backward on one leg for 10 to 30 meters. The forward hops should be characterized by low amplitude and little horizontal displacement. The backward hops should be more stiff-legged. The athlete's foot should be flat on contact in both directions.

Coaching Point: The athlete should spend the least amount of time on the ground as possible.

Drill #70: Forward Leg Springs With Chest Pass

Objective: To develop hip extension with eccentric loading

Equipment Needed: A shot put or medicine ball weighing four to eight pounds

Description: The athlete holds a weighted ball at his chest and springs forward off both legs and, upon landing, executes a chest pass to a partner or out into an open area. Three sets of five repetitions are recommended.

Coaching Points: Emphasize to the athlete the importance of the quality of his response with the ground. The athlete should land flat-footed and push through his hips while performing the chest pass.

Drill #71: Double-Leg Spring Forward With an Over-the-Back Throw

Objective: To stimulate the neuromuscular system; to work on exploding through the hips

Equipment Needed: A shot put or medicine ball weighing four to eight pounds

Description: The athlete springs forward on both legs, holding a weighted ball at his chest. He then lowers the ball between his legs and brings the weighted ball overhead to release it in an over-the-back throw. Three sets of five repetitions are recommended.

Coaching Point: The athlete should emphasize hip drive.

Drill #72: Double-Leg Spring Forward With an Underhand Forward Throw

Objective: To stimulate the neuromuscular system; to work on exploding through the hips

Equipment Needed: A shot put or medicine ball weighing four to eight pounds

Description: The athlete springs forward, followed immediately by an underhand forward throw. Three sets of five repetitions are recommended.

Coaching Point: The athlete should emphasize pushing through the hips as he throws.

Drill #73: Overhead Backward Throw Off a Box

Objective: To develop hip extension with an eccentric load

Equipment Needed: A shot put or medicine ball weighing four to eight pounds, a box (6 to 12 inches high for females; 12 to 18 inches high for males)

Description: The athlete holds the weighted ball at his chest and jumps backward off the box. When he contacts the ground, he lowers the ball between his legs and tosses the weight backward, releasing as the ball is directly overhead. Three sets of five repetitions are recommended.

Coaching Point: The athlete should emphasize pushing through the hips at the release.

Drill #74: Underhand Forward Throw Off a Box

Objective: To develop hip extension with an eccentric load

Equipment Needed: A shot put or medicine ball weighing four to eight pounds, a box (6 to 12 inches high for females; 12 to 18 inches high for males)

Description: The athlete holds the ball at his chest and jumps off the box, bringing the ball between his legs and releasing it forward. Three sets of five repetitions are recommended.

Coaching Point: See that the athlete lands flat-footed and pushes through his hips.

Drill #75: Over-the-Back Throw Off a Box

Objective: To develop hip extension with an eccentric load

Equipment Needed: A shot put or medicine ball weighing four to eight pounds, a box (6 to 12 inches high for females; 12 to 18 inches high for males)

Description: The athlete holds the ball at his chest and jumps backward off the box. When he contacts the ground, the ball is lowered between his legs and he tosses the weight backward, releasing as the ball is directly overhead. Three sets of five repetitions are recommended.

Coaching Point: See that the athlete lands flat-footed and explodes through his hips.

Drill #76: Lateral Forward Jumps in Sand

Objective: To strengthen the feet, ankles, and lower legs

Equipment Needed: A sand pit

Description: The athlete jumps from side to side in the sand pit, moving in a forward direction for a distance of 10 to 20 meters.

Coaching Points: The athlete should perform this drill barefoot. Make sure the athlete's lateral jumps are explosive and continuous.

Drill #77: Forward-Forward-Back in Sand

Objective: To build leg strength

Equipment Needed: A sand pit

Description: The athlete stands in a sand pit and springs forward two times, then immediately jumps backward for 30 meters.

Coaching Points: This drill uses forward and backward momentum to overload the leg muscles. Make sure the athlete's jumps are explosive and continuous.

Drill #78: Counter Movement Jump

Objective: To execute a vertical jump with eccentric loading, thus building explosive power in the legs and hips

Equipment Needed: None

Description: The athlete begins in a standing position. The athlete lowers his body into a squat position. Upon reaching the extent of the squat position, he immediately jumps vertically, as high as possible. Three sets of 10 repetitions are recommended.

Coaching Points: The depth of the squat for each athlete should approximate the depth of the weighted squats performed individually during strength training.

Drill #79: Three-Step Vertical Jump

Objective: To develop jumping power off one leg

Equipment Needed: A Vertec measuring device

Description: The athlete takes three running steps and jumps as high as possible off one leg. Three to four repetitions are recommended.

Coaching Points: This drill uses momentum to overload the leg muscles. Compare the athlete's standing vertical jump with his three-step vertical jump. Successful high jumpers are athletes with a six-inch or greater difference in height between these two efforts.

Drill #80: Box Jump

Objective: To develop jumping power

Equipment Needed: A box (14 to 18 inches high for women; 24 to 36 inches high for men)

Description: The athlete begins on the ground and jumps up onto the box, planting both feet simultaneously. Three sets of 10 repetitions are recommended.

Coaching Points: This drill can be done beginning from a static position or by using a counter movement. Remind the athlete to fire from the hips.

Drill #81: Drop Jumps

Objective: To develop reactive strength

Equipment Needed: Several boxes (ranging from 8 to 31 inches high)

Description: The athlete stands on top of the shortest box with his toes hanging over the edge. He then drops off the box with both feet together, landing flat-footed and rebounding off the ground as high as possible. The height of the box should be increased until the athlete begins to increase ground contact time. Three sets of 5 to 10 repetitions are recommended.

Coaching Point: The athlete should apply as large a force as possible in the shortest possible.

8

Drills With Hurdles

Hurdles may be used extensively as part of a jumper's training program. Hurdles can be used either as barriers to jump over or as instruments in mobility or flexibility exercises. The hurdle drills in this chapter are particularly good for developing rhythm and flexibility associated with the high-jump event. Following is an example of a hurdle mobility routine.

Hurdle Mobility Routine

The athlete should perform each of the following exercises through a series of 10 hurdles, placed close together:
- Continuous stepovers (3 reps)
- Lateral stepovers (2 reps to each side, over the middle of the hurdle)
- Lateral single-leg stepovers on the side of the hurdle (2 reps on each side)
- Lateral double-leg stepovers on the side of the hurdle (2 reps on each side)

Drill #82: Continuous Stepovers

Objective: To increase coordination and hip strength

Equipment Needed: 10 hurdles

Description: The athlete walks through a series of 10 hurdles (placed one after the other), stepping over each hurdle one leg at a time. One to two repetitions of this drill are recommended.

Coaching Points: The athlete should step over the middle of each hurdle with a controlled movement. This drill is good for balance and core strength.

Drill #83: Lateral Stepovers

Objective: To develop hip flexors and abductors

Equipment Needed: 10 hurdles

Description: The athlete walks sideways through a series of 10 hurdles, stepping laterally over each hurdle one leg at a time. One to two repetitions of this drill are recommended.

Coaching Point: Have the athlete increase the speed of his stepovers as he becomes more comfortable with the drill.

Drill #84: Hurdle Taps

Objective: To increase hip mobility and strength

Equipment Needed: A hurdle

Description: The athlete stands sideways to the hurdle. He brings one leg just over the top of the hurdle and taps the ground with his foot, then continues lifting his leg and tapping his foot from one side of the hurdle to the other. Ten to fifteen repetitions of this drill are recommended on both sides.

Coaching Point: Emphasize to the athlete the importance of quick foot contact from one side to the other.

Drill #85: Takeoffs Over a Hurdle

Objective: To teach proper firing of the takeoff leg

Equipment Needed: A hurdle

Description: The athlete skips or dribbles toward a hurdle, executing a high-jump takeoff in front of the hurdle. The athlete keeps his body erect, with his takeoff leg remaining as straight as possible, as he passes over the top of the hurdle. The athlete should land on his takeoff leg on the other side of the hurdle. Three to five sets of five repetitions are recommended.

Coaching Point: Make sure the barrier is low enough so the athlete feels confident remaining erect and keeping his takeoff leg straight as he passes over the barrier.

Drill #86: Hurdle Hamstring Massage

Objective: To release tension in the hamstring muscles

Equipment Needed: A hurdle

Description: The hurdle should be set to a height that will put the athlete's thigh at a 90-degree angle with the body when the thigh is placed on top of the hurdle. The athlete places the middle of his hamstring on top of the hurdle, and swings the lower leg from side to side, thereby massaging the body of the hamstring muscle. This should be done until tension is sufficiently released.

Coaching Point: This drill can be used in a warm-up or warm-down routine.

Drill #87: Hamstring Stretch on a Hurdle

Objective: To stretch the hamstring and inner-hip area

Equipment Needed: A hurdle

Description: The hurdle should be set to a height that will put the athlete's leg at a 90-degree angle with the body when the foot is placed on top of the hurdle. The athlete places the Achilles area of his foot on top of the hurdle. The athlete then rotates his leg from side to side, keeping his leg slightly bent at the knee. Three sets of 10 repetitions are recommended.

Coaching Point: Have the athlete keep his leg straight and his foot in the dorsiflexed position as he rotates his leg back and forth.

Drill #88: Pop Offs Over Barriers

Objective: To teach quality ground contact and flat-footed contact

Equipment Needed: Hurdles (6 to 18 inches high)

Description: The athlete pops off over a series of barriers. In between barriers, the athlete should make two flat-footed contacts. Three sets of 5 to 10 repetitions are recommended.

Coaching Points: Make sure the athlete's contacts are flat and quick. This drill is used to exercise the takeoff mechanism, specifically moving over the penultimate foot.

9

Drills With Balance Apparatus

Balance drills are very beneficial in strengthening the muscles and connective tissue, which enables the athlete to obtain and maintain good postural positions. The balance drills in this chapter are important to use as injury-prevention exercises.

Drill #89: Around the Worlds

Objective: To develop balance; to strengthen the stabilizer muscles around the ankle

Equipment Needed: Weighted ball (optional)

Description: The athlete balances on one leg. Using both hands, the athlete touches eight points in a half circle on the floor around his body in one direction, and then he touches eight points in the opposite direction. Two to three sets on each leg are recommended.

Coaching Points: The athlete should use slow, controlled movements to help maintain balance as he reaches out to each point. Once the athlete masters this drill, he can hold a weighted ball in his hands and touch each point with the ball.

Drill #90: Physioball March on Shoulders

Objective: To develop core strength

Equipment Needed: A physioball

Description: The athlete rests his shoulders on the physioball with his feet flat on the floor and his knees bent at a 90-degree angle. The athlete brings one bent knee up at a time in a marching movement. Three sets of 10 repetitions are recommended.

Coaching Point: The athlete should concentrate on balance and core-body stability.

Drill #91: Back Hypers on a Physioball

Objective: To strengthen the lower back and abdominals

Equipment Needed: A physioball

Description: The athlete lies with his stomach on the physioball and raises his upper body to just above parallel to a back-hyper position. Three sets of 10 to 15 repetitions are recommended.

Coaching Point: Make sure the athlete goes through the motion slowly, concentrating on the lower back and abdominal muscles.

Drill #92: Balance on a Physioball

Objective: To develop better balance and core strength

Equipment Needed: A physioball

Description: The athlete balances on his knees on top of a physioball, holding the position for one minute or longer. This drill should be repeated three times.

Coaching Points: When the athlete is on top of the ball, he should stay up on his knees and refrain from sitting on his ankles. This drill can be timed to mark progress.

Drill #93: Balance on Knees With Toss

Objective: To develop better balance and core strength

Equipment Needed: A physioball, a partner

Description: The athlete balances on top of a physioball as described in Drill #91. A partner throws a small, weighted ball to the athlete in various locations. The athlete catches the ball and throws it back to the partner with one hand. Three sets of 10 repetitions with each hand are recommended.

Coaching Points: This drill is excellent for core strength and balance and is most effective after Drill #91 is mastered.

Drill #94: Lying on Back With Marching

Objective: To develop core strength and lower back strength

Equipment Needed: None

Description: The athlete lies flat on his back and, using slow, controlled movements, performs a marching action, bringing one knee to his chest and then the other. Three sets of 10 repetitions are recommended.

Coaching Points: The athlete should pause with his knee in the marching position as a variation of this drill. The athlete should focus on pushing his belly button down toward the spine and keeping it in this stable position for inhalation and exhalation.

10

Supplemental Exercises

Supplemental drills can be integrated into warm-ups, circuits, and warm-downs in a workout program. These exercises are geared toward strengthening ligaments, stretching muscles, and strengthening connective tissue, thereby reducing the athlete's chance of injury.

Exercises using a stretchy, elastic band (e.g., a Thera-Band®) are particularly useful. These apparatuses can either be purchased pre-made at sporting goods stores or online, or they can be made using therapeutic rubber bands found in medical stores. To make your own, simply loop the band around both feet with a few inches to spare, then tie it off tightly. The drills in this chapter using an elastic band are particularly good for individuals who have tight hips or piriformis-muscle issues. If an athlete's hip strength is weak in adduction and abduction, the elastic band will be beneficial.

Many high-jump athletes need to address tight muscles in the hips and feet that are difficult to reach on their own. By using a small, hard ball such as a baseball, softball, or lacrosse ball, the athlete can perform self-massage and acupressure to loosen tight muscles resulting from such an impact-oriented and unilateral event.

Drill #95: Side Walks

Objective: To increase abductor strength and hip stability

Equipment Needed: An elastic band with medium to heavy resistance

Description: The athlete stands with his feet together and the elastic band tied around his ankles. He bends his knees slightly and steps to one side, pulling the band with force. The athlete then brings his feet back together. Three sets of 10 to 15 repetitions to each side are recommended.

Coaching Points: Make sure the athlete's feet are facing forward and he does not drag his foot when bringing it to meet his other foot. The athlete should have a slight bend in his knees while performing this exercise.

Drill #96: Forward Lateral Walks

Objective: To increase abductor strength and hip stability

Equipment Needed: An elastic band with medium to heavy resistance

Description: The athlete stands with his feet together and the elastic band tied around his ankles. He takes a forward, diagonal step with one foot, and then brings the back foot up to meet the front foot. He repeats the same step with the other foot to the other side, continuing in a zigzag pattern. Three sets of 10 to 15 steps to each side are recommended.

Coaching Points: Make sure the athlete's feet are facing forward and he does not drag his foot when bringing it to meet his other foot. The athlete should have a slight bend in his knees while performing this exercise.

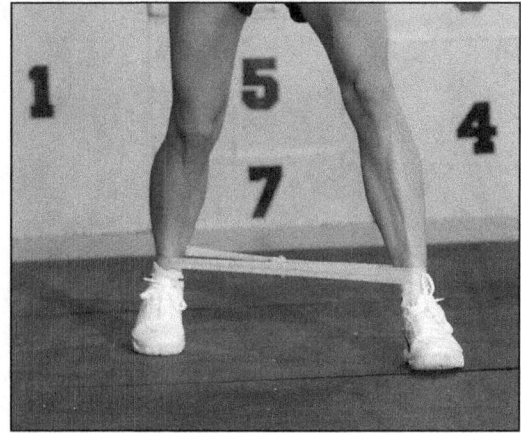

Drill #97: Hamstring Curl

Objective: To strengthen the hamstrings

Equipment Needed: An elastic band

Description: The athlete ties one end of the elastic band to a stable point near floor-level. He ties the other end of the band around his foot. From a standing position, the athlete then performs a hamstring curl. Three sets of 10 repetitions are recommended.

Coaching Point: Make sure the athlete fires the hamstring muscle quickly, bringing his ankle to the buttocks and back down.

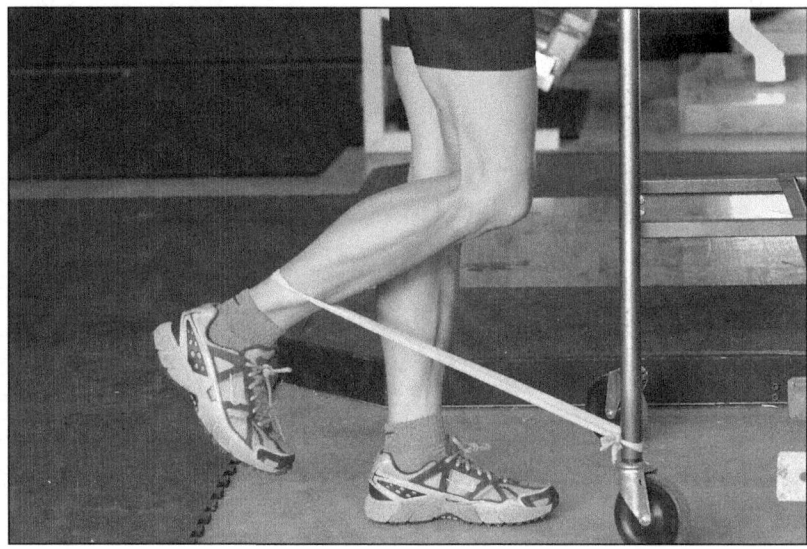

Drill #98: Piriformis Massage

Objective: To loosen the hip-area muscles; to relieve piriformus pressure and sciatic nerve pain

Equipment Needed: A small, hard ball (e.g., a baseball or softball)

Description: The athlete places a small ball in his hip pocket and sits on the ground on top of it, allowing his body weight to control the amount of pressure against the ball. The athlete rolls his body in both a clockwise and a counterclockwise motion. Thirty seconds to one minute of massage on each hip is recommended.

Coaching Points: This exercise relaxes the muscles that abduct and externally rotate the thigh. This exercise is especially good for athletes with piriformis-related problems, common with the high-jump event.

Drill #99: Foot Massage With a Ball

Objective: To increase blood flow; to help remove muscle tension in the feet

Equipment Needed: A small, hard ball (e.g., a baseball, softball, or lacrosse ball)

Description: The athlete sits in a chair barefoot. He places a small ball under his foot and applies pressure to the ball with his body weight. The athlete should roll the ball lengthwise down his foot. Thirty seconds to one minute of massage per foot is recommended.

Coaching Points: This exercise can be used for athletes with plantar fascitis, arch strain, or foot cramps, or simply for revitalizing the foot.

Drill #100: Bridge

Objective: To strengthen and increase back and abdominal flexibility

Equipment Needed: None

Description: Starting in a supine position, the athlete bends his knees with the soles of his feet placed firmly on the ground and his arms at his side. He then slowly pushes the pelvis upward, curling the tailbone under, until the back is arched into a bridge. As the athlete comes down, he exhales coming down from the top of the spine, one vertebra at a time, until the back rests flat on the ground. Two to three sets of eight repetitions are recommended.

Coaching Point: The athlete's legs and hips should do most of the work.

Drill #101: Barefoot Walks

Objective: To strengthen the feet, ankles, and lower legs

Equipment Needed: None

Description: The athlete walks barefoot with the following foot positions: on his heels, on his toes, inverted, everted, toes in, and toes out. Two repetitions walking a distance of 10 meters are recommended.

Coaching Points: This drill can be included as part of a warm-down. This drill can be done on a solid surface or in the sand.

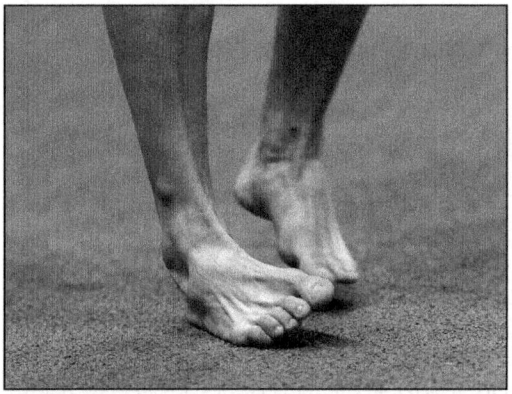
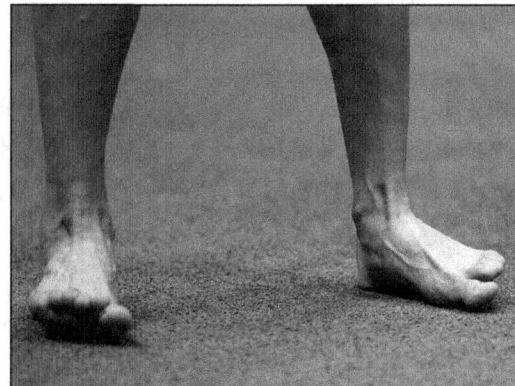
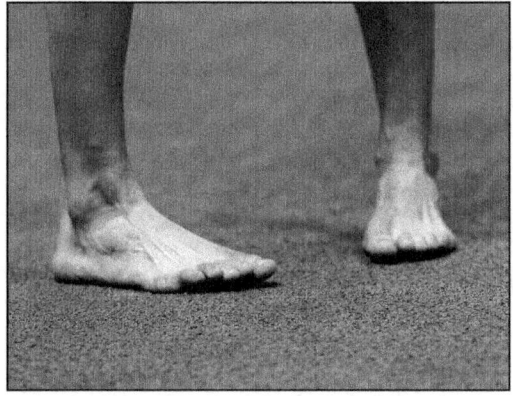
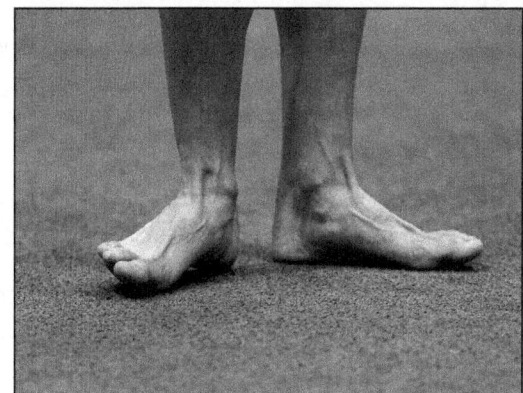

References and Recommended Reading

Badon, T. (1988). Constructing and utilizing the "ultimate" jump ramp. *Track Technique*, 106, 3378-3380.

Bompa, T. O. (1999). *Periodization Training for Sports*. Champaign, Ill.: Human Kinetics.

Bompa, T. O. (1994). *Periodization: Theory and Methodology of Training* (4th ed.). Champaign, Ill.: Human Kinetics.

Chu, D. (1998). *Jumping Into Plyometrics*. (2nd ed.). Champaign, Ill.: Human Kinetics.

Csikszentmihalyi, M. & Jackson, S. (1999). *Flow in Sports: The Keys to Optimal Experiences and Performances*. Champaign, Ill.: Human Kinetics.

Ecker, T. (1985). *Basic Track & Field Biomechanics* (2nd ed.). Los Altos, Calif.: Track & Field News Press.

Freeman, W. H. (2001). *Peak When It Counts: Periodization for American Track & Field*. Mountain View, Calif.: Track & Field News Press.

Gordon, B. & Dapena, J. (1999). *Women's High Jump #19*. Scientific Services Project. USA Track & Field. Biomechanics Laboratory, Dept. of Kinesiology, Indiana University.

Jacoby, E. & Fraley, B. (1995). *Complete Book of Jumps*. Champaign, Ill.: Human Kinetics.

Kogler, A. (1995). *Yoga for Every Athlete: Secrets of an Olympic Coach*. St. Paul, Minn.: Llewellyn Publications.

McGill, S. (2007). *Low Back Disorders: Evidence-Based prevention and Rehabilitation*. (2nd ed.). Champaign, Ill.: Human Kinetics.

Orlick, T. (1980). *In Pursuit of Excellence: How to Win in Sport and Life Through Mental Training* (2nd ed.). Champaign, Ill.: Human Kinetics.

Verstegen, M. & Williams, P. (2005). *The Core Performance: The Revolutionary Workout Program to Transform Your Body and Your Life*. Emmaus, Pa.: Rodale Books.

Additional Resources

USATF Coaching Schools, Levels I, II & III, www.usatf.org

Recommended Videos

Rovelto, C. (2012). *Cliff Rovelto's Complete Guide to the High Jump*. Ames, Iowa: Championship Productions.

Wentland, G. (2004). *Perfecting the High Jump Approach*. Monterey, Calif.: Coaches Choice.

Wentland, G. (2004). *Effective Practice Drills for the High Jump*. Monterey, Calif.: Coaches Choice.

About the Authors

Cliff Rovelto is an internationally recognized authority in jumps and combined events. He has coached collegians for over 32 years. In his position as the director of track and field at Kansas State University, he has personally coached 56 athletes who have earned a combined total of 136 NCAA All-American certificates, and has coached 82 conference individual event champions. He was the 2001 U.S. Track Coaches Association National Coach of the Year and five-time Midwest Region Coach of the Year. He has also been a two-time Big 12 Conference Coach of the Year. In 2004, he was awarded the United States Women's Track and Field College Coaches Award for Service.

Rovelto has assisted with curriculum development for the USA combined-events coaching education program and also served as an instructor for the program. He is one of only two coaches in the United States to coach multiple combined-event athletes to over 8,000 (men) and 6,000 (women) points.

Rovelto has coached 14 individual Olympians, who have competed in the games on 18 occasions—six of these athletes have been high jumpers. At the 2004 Olympics in Athens, Greece, one of his athletes, Matt Hemingway, was a silver medalist, and another, Jamie Nieto, placed fourth. In 2012, all three men's team USA high jumpers were coached by Rovelto. Erik Kynard, a senior at Kansas State, won an Olympic silver medal. Another of Rovelto's athletes, Jesse Williams, won the 2011 IAAF World Championship title in the high jump. Rovelto has also coached 18 USA indoor and outdoor senior national champions in the high jump. While at Kansas State, he has coached 23 Big 12 Conference champions, 49 All-Americans, and seven NCAA individual champions in the high jump.

Rovelto has served as the coach of the USA decathlon team in dual meets with Germany in 1997 and 2003. He was an assistant coach for the 2003 World Outdoor Track and Field Championships in Paris, France, the 2005 World Outdoor Track and Field Championships in Helsinki, Finland, and the 2007 team that competed in Osaka, Japan. He also served as an assistant on the World Cup staff in 2002. In 2011, he was the head men's coach for the USA Pan American team and also served on the America's team staff for the IAAF Continental Cup in Splot, Croatia.

Gwen Wentland was a world-class high jumper with more than 18 years of competitive experience. She was ranked by Track & Field News as one of the nation's top 10 high jumpers for 15 years. Wentland has two national high-jump titles and three runner-up finishes to her name. She is also a former world-record holder in the pentathlon high jump at 6'4 1/4", and the American-record holder in the heptathlon high jump at 6'4". She was a member of the 2003 U.S. World Championship team that competed in Paris, France

Wentland has served as the 2012 Olympic Games assistant coach for jumps and combined events in London, England. She was the assistant coach for the 2010 World Indoor Championships in Doha, Qatar, 2002 World junior Championships in Kingston, Jamaica, and worked as the Athletes Liaison Officer for the 2001 World Championships in Debrecen, Hungary, Greece, and the 1997 World Championships in Athens, Greece. She has served as an assistant coach at both her alma mater, Kansas State University, and the University of California, Irvine. In 2006, Wentland was inducted into the Kansas State University Athletic Hall of Fame.